WNBA Champions

BY ELLEN LABRECQUE

2018 WNBA champion Seattle Storm ▶

Published by The Child's World®
1980 Lookout Drive • Mankato, MN 56003-1705
800-599-READ • www.childsworld.com

Photographs:
Cover: Kamil Krzaczynski/AP Images.
Interior: AP Images: Carolyn Kaster 2; Rich
Pedroncelli 5; Alex Brandon 6, 14; David J. Phillip
9; Jeff Wheeler/Minneapolis Star Tribune 10; Mark
J. Terrill, 13; Matt Marton 18; Cal Sport Media 21.
Imagn/USA Today Sports: Brad Mills 17.

ISBN 9781503835313
LCCN 2019944744

Printed in the United States of America

Contents

The Best of the Best

The most exciting WNBA game ever was on October 20, 2016. It was Game 5 of the WNBA Finals. The Los Angeles Sparks played the Minnesota Lynx. The best-of-five series was tied 2–2. Three seconds remained. The Lynx led 76–75. Sparks **forward** Nneka Ogwumike grabbed an offensive **rebound**. She hit the game-winning shot with three seconds to go! The Sparks won, 77–76. Let's meet other great WNBA champions!

WNBA champions get to hold up this large trophy for winning the WNBA Finals. The smaller, glass trophy goes to the WNBA Finals Most Valuable Player (MVP). ▶

Washington Mystics

One fact was certain—there would be a first-time WNBA champion in 2019. Both teams in that year's WNBA Finals were after their first title. After five exciting games, the Washington Mystics were the champs! They won the final game over the Connecticut Sun, 89–78. Washington star Elena Delle Donne had 21 points. Her teammate, Emma Meesseman, had 22. "I'm very happy to be one of the players who brought this team its first championship," said Delle Donne.

In the 2019 WNBA Finals, Elena Delle Donne (in red) wore a mask to protect a broken nose.

Houston Comets

The Comets are the only WNBA team to win four titles in a row (1997–2000). They were led by the "big three"—Cynthia Cooper, Sheryl Swoopes, and Tina Thompson. The Comets were the first great WNBA team. "We made people stand up and watch," said Thompson. Winning was awesome, but the Comets also faced heartbreak.

Point guard Kim Perrot died of cancer during their third season. The players **dedicated** their last two titles to their former teammate.

Team:
Houston Comets

Championship Titles:
4 (1997, 1998, 1999, 2000)

WNBA Seasons:
1997–2008

Kim Perrot celebrated two titles with Houston. ▶

Minnesota Lynx

Team:
Minnesota Lynx

Championship Titles:
4 (2011, 2013, 2015, 2017)

Years in League:
1999–Present

T he Lynx are the only current WNBA team to win four championships. (The Comets are no longer in the league.) In their first championship series in 2011, they were behind at halftime in every game! They **rallied** back in each game to **sweep** the Atlanta Dream! Minnesota's star was Maya Moore. Moore led her team to the WNBA Finals six times in seven seasons from 2011 to 2017. What's their key to winning? "We just have fun together," says Moore.

Win the WNBA title, get a parade! The Lynx enjoyed four parades. Sylvia Fowles (left) and Maya Moore showed fans the team's trophies in 2017.

Los Angeles Sparks

Team:
Los Angeles Sparks

Championship Titles:
3 (2001, 2002, 2016)

Years in League:
1997–Present

The Sparks ended the Houston Comets' great run. Los Angeles beat the four-time champs in 2001. The Sparks won the title again in 2002. Nikki Teasley clinched their second title. She hit a **three-pointer** with 2.1 seconds left in the final game. The Sparks won 69–66. The Sparks had to wait another 14 years to win their third title. In 2016, they beat the powerful Minnesota Lynx. They had to play in Minneapolis. Still, the Sparks upset the Lynx in Game 5. They squeaked out a last-second, one-point victory!

Candace Parker was the big star for the Sparks during their 2016 title run. ▶

Detroit Shock

Team:
Detroit Shock

Championship Titles:
3 (2003, 2006, 2008)

Years in League:
1998-2009

The Detroit Shock is the only WNBA team to go from worst to first. In 2002, they finished last with a 9–23 record. In 2003, they finished the regular season 25–9. What a turnaround! Detroit was the **underdog** when it faced the Los Angeles Sparks. The final game was played in front of 22,076 fans in Detroit. That was the biggest crowd in WNBA history! **Center** Ruth Riley scored 27 points. The Shock shocked the Sparks and won 83–78. Detroit went on to win two more titles.

Detroit's WNBA champions presented President Barack Obama with a team jersey when he welcomed them at the White House.

Seattle Storm

Team:
Seattle Storm

Championship Titles:
3 (2004, 2010, 2018)

Years in League:
2000-Present

Who was part of all three of the Storm's titles? Point guard Sue Bird. Coaches changed. Teammates changed. Bird never flew away. Does Bird have a favorite of the three championships? "Each is special in its own way," she says. The most recent is one the most memorable, though. "I didn't even know I'd still be playing at that point." At 38, Bird was the oldest player in the league. She had 10 **assists** in the final game of the 2018 series.

Seattle's Crystal Langhorne gathered her teammates for a championship selfie in 2018. ▶

Phoenix Mercury

The Mercury was one of the eight original WNBA teams. Since then, they have swooped up three titles. The heart of the team is guard Diana Taurasi. Playing with the Mercury since 2004, she led them to all three titles. During the best-of-five series in 2014, the Mercury beat the Chicago Sky 3–0. Taurasi was named the WNBA Finals MVP. She scored 24 points in the final game.

Team:
Phoenix Mercury

Championship Titles:
3 (2007, 2009, 2014).

Years in League:
1997–Present

At 6'9" (2.05 m), Brittney Griner stood tall as a player and as the 2014 champ.

Sacramento Monarchs and Indiana Fever

The Monarchs started in 1997. The team won its only championship in 2005. It beat the Connecticut Sun. Yolanda "Yo Yo" Griffith of the Monarchs **averaged** 18.5 points and 9.8 rebounds. She was the Finals MVP. The Fever scorched their way to their first title in 2012. In the WNBA Finals, they defeated the **defending champion** Minnesota Lynx. In the fourth and final game, Indiana won 87–78.

Team:
Sacramento Monarchs

Championship Titles:
1 (2005)

Years in League:
1997–2009

Team:
Indiana Fever

Championship Titles:
1 (2012)

Years in League:
2000–Present

Indiana's Tammy Sutton-Brown, Katie Douglas, and Tamika Catchings (left to right) show off their brand-new 2012 championship T-shirts.

Glossary

assist (uh-SIST) a pass that helps a teammate score a basket

averaged (AV-uh-rijd) in sports, reached a similar number over time

center (SEN-ter) the tallest player on a team, she usually plays closest to the basket

dedicated (DED-ih-kay-ted) honored in another's memory

defending champion (deh-FEND-ing CHAMP-ee-un) the team that most recently was the best in the league

forward (FOR-werd) a position that plays near the basket and often scores and rebounds

point guard (POYNT GARD) the basketball player who directs the offense

rallied (RALL-eed) came from behind to win

rebound (REE-bownd) to grab the ball after a missed shot

sweep (SWEEP) in sports, to win all of the games in a short series

three-pointer (THREE-POYNT-er) a basket made from outside an arc on the court, worth three points

underdog (UN-der-dog) a team or a player who is not expected to win

Find Out More

IN THE LIBRARY

Delle Donne, Elena. *Full-Court Press*. New York, NY:
Harper Entertainment, 2018.
(Note: This is a novel by the Washington Mystics' star player.)

Levit, Joe. *Basketball's G.O.A.T.: Michael Jordan,
LeBron James, and More (Sports' Greatest of All
Time)*. New York, NY: Lerner Publishing, 2019.

Sports Illustrated Kids. *My First Book of Basketball*.
New York, NY: Sports Illustrated Kids, 2018.

ON THE WEB

Visit our Web site for links about the
WNBA champions:
childsworld.com/links

Note to Parents, Teachers, and Librarians:
We routinely verify our Web links to make sure they are safe
and active sites. So encourage your readers to check them out!

Index

About the Author

Ellen Labrecque has written more than 100 books for children. A former editor at *Sports Illustrated Kids* Magazine, she loves covering and watching the WNBA. She played basketball in college, where she was named to the Academic All-America team. She lives in Bucks County, Pennsylvania, with her husband and two kids.